DOBERMANS AT HEART

THE PERFECT FAMILY DOGS

STACEY SANCHEZ

Copyright © 2023 Stacey Sanchez

All rights reserved. This publication, or any part thereof, may not be reproduced in any form or by any means, including electronic, photographic, or mechanical, or by any sound recording system, or by any device for storage and retrieval of information, without the written permission of the copyright owner.

Contents

About the Author 5

Chapter 1: Introduction to Dobermans 8

    Doberman Pinschers Are Often Portrayed as Aggressive Dogs, but in Reality, They Are Excellent Family Dogs. ... 9

    History of Doberman Pinscher 12

    Physical Characteristics of Doberman Pinscher 15

Chapter 2: Temperament and Behavior Characteristics .. 18

    Intelligence and Trainability 21

    How Dobermans Interact With Children 24

    Benefits of Having a Doberman as a Family Dog 26

Chapter 3: Doberman's Loyalty and Protection 30

    Doberman's Loyalty Towards Their Family 31

How Dobermans Can Provide Protection for Their Families 33

Health and Maintenance 36

Chapter 4: Common Health Issues for Dobermans 37

Tips for Maintaining Your Doberman's Health 41

Chapter 5: Doberman Breeding 46

Breed Characteristics 47

Popularity and Recognition 50

Chapter 6: Training and Socialization 54

Importance of Training and Socialization for Dobermans
.... 54

Effective Training and Socialization Methods 57

Chapter 7: Misconceptions and Controversies Surrounding Dobermans 62

Common Misconceptions 63

Controversies Surrounding Dobermans 66

Conclusion 69

Final Thoughts and Recommendations for Potential Doberman Owners 73

About the Author

Stacey Sanchez is a dedicated Doberman Pinscher Dog breeder with an unwavering commitment to upholding the highest standards in breed quality. With over 15 years of experience as a Doberman owner, Stacey has developed an intimate understanding of the breed's unique traits and characteristics, allowing her to produce exceptional litters that embody the true essence of these majestic canines.

In addition to her extensive involvement with Dobermans,

Stacey boasts over 20 years of experience working with various dog breeds, honing her expertise in canine care and training. Her deep-rooted passion for animals extends far beyond the realm of breeding, as she wholeheartedly embraces a nurturing and compassionate approach to all creatures, great and small.

Residing in the vibrant state of Florida, Stacey leads a fulfilling life surrounded by her family and her beloved Doberman companions. Her bond with her dogs is unbreakable, and she cherishes the shared adventures and everyday moments spent with them. Stacey's innate ability to connect with animals, coupled with her genuine love for them, creates an environment of trust, respect, and unending affection.

When Stacey isn't tending to her dogs or spending time with her family, she enjoys venturing out on errands with her Dobermans by her side. This not only showcases her commitment to responsible pet ownership but also serves as a testament to her desire to integrate her passion seamlessly into every aspect of her life.

Stacey Sanchez's unwavering dedication to preserving the integrity of the Doberman Pinscher breed, coupled with her boundless love for animals, makes her a truly remarkable and compassionate individual within the world of dog breeding.

Chapter 1:

Introduction to Dobermans

Dobermans are frequently labeled as aggressive guard dogs, but contrary to this stereotype, they possess the ability to become affectionate and devoted family companions. These elegant and intelligent dogs display remarkable adaptability and excel in diverse roles, including police and military work, as well as therapy and service animals. Unfortunately, their suitability as a family dog is often underestimated.

In this book, we will explore the numerous reasons why Dobermans stand out as the ultimate family dog. Through an in-depth examination, we will uncover their affectionate and energetic nature, as well as their innate protective instincts. These exceptional canines encompass all the qualities required to be outstanding companions for families of any size.

We will delve into the rich history, distinctive characteristics, and temperament of Dobermans to gain a comprehensive understanding of why they excel as remarkable family pets. Additionally, we will offer practical tips and valuable advice on selecting, training, and caring for a Doberman, ensuring a joyful and thriving life together for both you and your beloved canine companion.

Whether you are contemplating adding a Doberman to your family or are already a proud owner, this book will equip you with the essential knowledge to foster a fulfilling relationship with this exceptional breed. So, sit back, relax, and prepare to uncover why Dobermans truly stand out as the finest choice for a family dog.

Doberman Pinschers Are Often Portrayed as Aggressive Dogs, but in Reality, They Are Excellent Family Dogs.

Here are some reasons why:

Loyalty: Dobermans demonstrate exceptional loyalty towards their families, showing a deep devotion and a strong desire to safeguard their loved ones. Their protective instincts drive them to go to great lengths to ensure the safety and well-being of their family members. This unwavering loyalty is a key factor that contributes to their reputation as outstanding family dogs.

Intelligence: Dobermans rank among the most intelligent dog breeds, showcasing remarkable cognitive abilities. They possess a keen intellect, enabling them to grasp commands quickly and exhibit great obedience when appropriately trained. Their high level of intelligence not only makes them highly trainable but also allows them to understand and respond effectively to their family's expectations and desires.

Energy Level: Dobermans have a moderate to high energy level, making them ideal companions for families with active lifestyles. Their zest for play and exercise requires regular physical activity to ensure their well-being and happiness. This makes them a perfect match for families who enjoy activities such as walks, hikes, or runs as part of their daily routine.

Affectionate: Dobermans also possess a deep affection for their families, displaying a genuine longing for closeness and physical connection. They delight in cuddling and being in close proximity to their loved ones, making them exceptional pets for families seeking a loyal and affectionate companion to share precious moments and create lasting bonds.

Protective: Dobermans have earned a well-deserved reputation as exceptional guard dogs. They possess a natural instinct to protect their families and are willing to defend them against perceived threats. This inherent protective nature makes them outstanding family dogs, as they remain vigilant in safeguarding their loved ones at all times.

Good with kids: Dobermans generally exhibit positive behavior towards children. They demonstrate gentleness and patience when interacting with kids, which contributes to their suitability as excellent family dogs. However, it is crucial to supervise interactions between young children and dogs to ensure safety and prevent any potential accidents.

In conclusion, Doberman Pinschers truly excel as family dogs, thanks to their exceptional traits of loyalty, intelligence, energy level, affectionate nature, protectiveness, and positive temperament with children. However, it is crucial to conduct thorough research and carefully consider whether a Doberman aligns with your family's lifestyle and requirements before welcoming one into your home. Taking the time to make an informed decision will ensure a harmonious and fulfilling relationship between your family and this remarkable breed.

History of Doberman Pinscher

Once upon a time, nestled within the rich tapestry of canine history, there emerged a breed that would captivate hearts and leave an indelible mark on the world of dogs. This is the story of the Doberman Pinscher, a breed that originated in Germany during the late 19th century.

In the town of Apolda, a tax collector named Louis Dobermann sought a companion and protector that would accompany him during his daily rounds. Driven by his desire for a loyal and versatile working dog, he embarked on a journey to create a breed that would possess the ideal combination of intelligence, strength, and loyalty.

To achieve this vision, Louis Dobermann carefully selected and crossed several breeds, including the Rottweiler, German Pinscher, Weimaraner, and Greyhound, among others. Through meticulous breeding practices, he aimed to develop a dog that would be an ideal companion and guardian.

The resulting breed, initially known as the "Dobermann Pinscher" after its creator, quickly garnered attention for its exceptional qualities. The Doberman Pinscher possessed a regal and athletic appearance, marked by a sleek coat, a powerful physique, and an alert expression that exuded intelligence and confidence.

With its inherent loyalty, the Doberman Pinscher found favor not only as a protector of homes but also as a trusted companion for police and military personnel. Their innate drive, agility, and trainability made them valuable assets in law enforcement, search and rescue operations, and other important roles.

Over the years, the breed's popularity spread beyond Germany's borders, captivating the hearts of dog enthusiasts worldwide. As Dobermans became treasured family pets, their true nature as affectionate and devoted companions shone through. Families experienced firsthand the unwavering loyalty and gentle nature that coexisted with their protective instincts.

Despite their undeniable allure, Doberman Pinschers have had to overcome unjust stereotypes perpetuated by media and misinformed portrayals. These stereotypes often portrayed them as aggressive dogs, overshadowing their true temperament and character. However, knowledgeable dog owners and enthusiasts have continued to champion the breed, promoting responsible ownership and showcasing the Doberman's true nature as a loving and devoted family companion.

Today, the legacy of Louis Dobermann lives on through the Doberman Pinscher. The breed's rich history is a testament to the power of human vision, dedication, and careful breeding practices. From its humble origins to its present status as a cherished breed, the Doberman Pinscher continues to bring joy, loyalty, and unwavering devotion to families fortunate enough to share their lives with these remarkable dogs.

Physical Characteristics of Doberman Pinscher

1. **Height:** Dobermans generally have a height ranging from 24 to 28 inches at the shoulder. It's worth noting that females tend to be slightly smaller in size compared to males.

2. **Weight:** The weight of Dobermans can vary based on their gender and individual size. Adult males typically weigh between 75 to 100 pounds, while females generally weigh between 60 to 90 pounds.

3. **Coat:** Dobermans boast a short and sleek coat that lies smoothly against their body. Their coat comes in a range of colors, including black, red, blue, and fawn. It's not uncommon for some Dobermans to have a

white patch on their chest or feet, adding an extra touch of uniqueness to their appearance.

4. **Head:** The Doberman possesses a distinct wedge-shaped head that is in proportion to its body. It is characterized by a long, muscular neck that seamlessly transitions into a broad chest, reflecting the breed's strength and elegance.

5. **Ears:** Traditionally, Doberman ears were commonly cropped, resulting in upright ears. However, it's important to note that this practice is becoming less prevalent. Many Dobermans today have natural ears, which naturally flop over, adding to their unique charm.

6. **Tail:** Traditionally, Dobermans had their tails docked, a practice where the tail is surgically shortened. However, it's important to note that tail docking is now illegal in some countries and is becoming less common in general.

7. **Eyes:** Dobermans typically have medium-sized, almond-shaped eyes that contribute to their alert and intelligent expression. The most common eye color in Dobermans is dark brown, further enhancing their

striking appearance.

8. **Gait:** The Doberman showcases a graceful and powerful gait. They move with a long and smooth stride, enabling them to cover considerable ground with remarkable agility and speed.

In conclusion, the Doberman Pinscher embodies an impressive and distinctive physical presence. This breed showcases a well-proportioned frame with a sleek and muscular build. Their coat is short and smooth, offering a range of captivating colors, while traditionally, their ears have been cropped and their tails docked, although these practices are now less common and subject to regional regulations.

Chapter 2:

Temperament and Behavior Characteristics

Doberman dogs are renowned for their remarkable appearance, intelligence, and unwavering loyalty to their owners. However, it is equally important to understand their temperament and behavior. In this chapter, we will delve deeper into the temperament and behavior traits of the Doberman dog breed.

Temperament

Dobermans are typically characterized as confident, alert, and obedient. They possess a keen intellect, making them quick learners and responsive to training. Additionally, their innate sense of loyalty drives them to be highly protective of their owners, often displaying territorial tendencies. This natural instinct also contributes to their aptitude as exceptional guard dogs.

Dobermans are renowned for their high energy levels, making them a breed that thrives on ample exercise and mental stimulation. Regular physical activity and mental engagement are crucial to their well-being. Without sufficient outlets for their energy, they may exhibit destructive behaviors and may develop various behavioral issues. However, with proper exercise and mental stimulation, Dobermans can exhibit a calm and well-behaved demeanor indoors. It is essential for owners to provide them with the necessary outlets to channel their energy and keep them mentally stimulated, fostering a balanced and contented Doberman companion.

Behavior

Dobermans are often referred to as "velcro dogs" due to their strong bond and attachment to their owners. They thrive on human companionship and have a deep desire to be close to their loved ones as much as possible. They do not fare well when left alone for extended periods of time. Prolonged periods of separation can lead to feelings of anxiety and the development of separation anxiety in Dobermans.

Additionally, Dobermans possess a natural instinct to protect their families. They have an innate drive to safeguard their territory and will go to great lengths to ensure the safety of their loved ones. This protective nature lends itself to their potential as excellent guard dogs. However, it is crucial for Dobermans to be properly socialized from an early age. Without proper socialization, they may become overly protective and exhibit aggression towards strangers.

It is important to recognize that each individual Doberman can have unique temperament and behavior traits. Like all dogs, their disposition and behavior can be influenced by a combination of genetic factors, environmental conditions, and socialization experiences. Prior to acquiring a Doberman, it is advisable to conduct thorough research on the breeder and meet the dog's parents whenever possible. This can provide valuable insights into the potential temperament and behavior of the Doberman you are considering.

In conclusion, Doberman dogs possess a confident and loyal temperament and are renowned for their protective nature. To maintain good behavior indoors, they require ample exercise and mental stimulation while also thriving on meaningful human interaction. The key to ensuring a well-behaved and contented Doberman as a cherished member of your family lies in providing them with proper socialization and training. By investing time and effort in their socialization and training, you can nurture their positive traits and cultivate a harmonious relationship that brings joy and fulfillment to both you and your Doberman companion.

Intelligence and Trainability

Doberman dogs are widely acknowledged as one of the most intelligent breeds in the canine world. They exhibit remarkable perceptiveness and possess a remarkable capacity for learning and problem-solving. Their high intelligence enables them to adapt swiftly to changes in their surroundings, demonstrating their innate flexibility.

The Doberman's intelligence is evident in their ability to perform complex tasks, which has made them invaluable in roles such as police and military work for many years. In fact, Stanley Coren, in his book "The Intelligence of Dogs," ranks Dobermans as the 5th most intelligent dog breed. In addition, their acute observational skills and heightened awareness of their environment further enhance their capabilities as exceptional watchdogs and guard dogs. They are quick to alert their owners to any unusual activity or environmental changes, exhibiting a strong sense of vigilance.

Doberman dogs exhibit a remarkable level of trainability and are renowned for their positive response to training methods that emphasize positive reinforcement. They possess a strong desire to please their owners and thoroughly enjoy the process of acquiring new skills and knowledge. Their inherent intelligence and aptitude for learning enable them to adapt swiftly to various training techniques and engage in a wide range of activities. Whether it is mastering obedience commands, participating in agility exercises, or excelling in protection sports, Dobermans demonstrate their versatility and capability.

Training plays a vital role in the development of Doberman dogs. Without proper training and socialization, they may exhibit destructive behaviors and develop behavioral issues. However, with consistent and positive training, they can become well-mannered and obedient companions. Dobermans possess a heightened sensitivity to their owners' emotions and body language, allowing them to readily discern subtle cues. As a result, they display remarkable responsiveness to training methods that employ positive reinforcement and reward-based techniques.

Doberman dogs showcase exceptional skills and aptitude in a range of dog sports, including obedience, agility, and protection sports. Their competitive spirit shines through as they enthusiastically engage in these activities.

Additionally, their calm and gentle nature has led to their utilization as therapy dogs. Being highly social animals, they relish spending time with their owners and fellow canines.

It is important to recognize that while Doberman dogs are highly trainable, they possess unique personalities and individual preferences when it comes to training. Some may exhibit greater motivation towards food rewards, while others may be more inclined towards play or verbal praise. Understanding and appreciating these individual traits is crucial for owners to achieve optimal results during training sessions.

In summary, Doberman dogs are characterized by their remarkable intelligence and trainability. Their propensity for learning and problem-solving enables them to adapt readily to diverse training techniques and activities. Proper training and socialization are paramount for cultivating their well-mannered and obedient nature. With consistent and positive guidance, Doberman dogs can become a superb addition to any family, enriching their lives with loyalty, companionship, and their impressive skills.

How Dobermans Interact With Children

Doberman dogs exemplify loyalty and an affectionate nature towards their families, including children. Their innate instinct to protect their loved ones renders them excellent watchdogs and guardians for youngsters. However, as with any dog breed, comprehending their behavior and taking appropriate precautions is vital to ensure the safety of both the child and the dog.

With proper socialization and training, Doberman dogs can exhibit gentleness and patience towards children. They possess a high tolerance for youngsters and can adjust their behavior based on the child's age and size. Nonetheless, due to their size and strength, accidental knocking over of small children can occur, potentially resulting in injuries. Consequently, it is crucial to closely supervise all interactions between children and Doberman dogs.

Socialization plays a vital role in ensuring positive interactions between your Doberman dog and children. Early socialization helps familiarize your dog with children and teaches them appropriate behavior. It is important to expose your dog to children of various ages and sizes, guiding them to interact in a positive and gentle manner.

Alongside socialization, training is crucial for Doberman dogs that interact with children. Positive reinforcement training methods can help your dog learn proper behavior and reinforce desirable habits. Teaching your dog basic obedience commands like "sit," "stay," and "come," as well as leash manners, promotes calmness and prevents accidental knocking over or excessive excitement around children.

Additionally, it is crucial to educate children on how to interact with dogs safely. They should be instructed to approach dogs calmly, avoiding rough play or behavior that may be perceived as threatening. Respecting the dog's personal space and refraining from hugging or pulling on the dog are essential guidelines. It is imperative to supervise children's interactions with the dog and address any inappropriate behavior promptly.

In conclusion, Doberman dogs can make excellent family pets when they receive proper socialization and training. Their innate protective nature can make them reliable watchdogs and guardians for children. However, it remains important to supervise interactions between children and Doberman dogs and take necessary precautions to ensure the safety of both parties. With appropriate training and socialization, Doberman dogs can become loving and loyal companions for families with children.

Benefits of Having a Doberman as a Family Dog

Doberman dogs are a sought-after breed renowned for their loyalty, intelligence, and protective instincts. Their exceptional qualities and characteristics make them outstanding additions to families, offering numerous advantages to those who decide to make them part of their households.

First and foremost, Dobermans are known for their unwavering loyalty. They form deep bonds with their human companions and are dedicated to protecting and being by their side. This loyalty extends to their immediate family members, whom they consider an integral part of their pack. The devotion and commitment they show to their owners create a strong and lasting bond, making them not just pets but true and trusted companions.

Here are some of the benefits of having a Doberman as a family dog:

1. Protection:

Dobermans are renowned for their innate protective instincts and have a long history of serving as guard dogs.

They exhibit unwavering loyalty towards their families and will go to great lengths to safeguard them from perceived threats. By having a Doberman in the household, families can enjoy an enhanced sense of security and peace of mind.

2. Affectionate Companions:

Dobermans possess a deeply affectionate nature and form strong bonds with their human companions. They thrive on companionship and enjoy spending quality time with their family members. Their loving and loyal demeanor makes them excellent playmates for children and devoted, affectionate companions for individuals of all ages.

3. Active Lifestyle:

Dobermans are a high-energy breed that thrives on physical activity and mental stimulation. Owning a Doberman can inspire families to adopt a more active lifestyle, engaging in regular exercise, walks, and outdoor activities alongside their canine companion. This promotes not only the physical well-being of both the dog and the family but also strengthens the bond between them.

4. Trainability:

Dobermans are renowned for their high intelligence and

trainability. They possess a keen desire to learn and are quick to pick up new commands and skills. Their exceptional trainability makes them an ideal choice for families seeking a dog that can easily grasp obedience training and excel in various activities such as agility or tracking. With consistent training and positive reinforcement, Dobermans can become well-behaved and highly skilled companions.

5. Adaptability:

Dobermans are remarkably adaptable dogs that can thrive in different living environments. Whether residing in urban areas or rural settings, Dobermans can adjust and flourish. They can comfortably adapt to various living arrangements, including apartments or larger homes, as long as their exercise and mental stimulation needs are met. This versatility makes them a suitable choice for families seeking a companion that can adapt to their lifestyle.

6. Low Maintenance:

Dobermans have short, easy-to-maintain coats that require minimal grooming. While they do shed, the shedding is not excessive, and regular brushing can help manage it effectively. This characteristic makes them an excellent choice for families seeking a low-maintenance dog in terms of grooming. With simple grooming routines and occasional bathing, Dobermans can maintain a tidy and well-groomed appearance.

Chapter 3:

Doberman's Loyalty and Protection

Doberman dogs are renowned for their unwavering loyalty and natural protective instincts. Their strong sense of loyalty makes them dedicated and devoted companions to their families, forming deep bonds that endure throughout their lives. When it comes to protection, Dobermans are instinctively vigilant and possess a strong desire to safeguard their loved ones. They are known for their courage and fearlessness when it comes to protecting their family and property. With their exceptional loyalty and protective nature, Dobermans provide a sense of security and unwavering devotion that is truly unparalleled.

Doberman's Loyalty Towards Their Family

Doberman dogs are renowned for their unwavering loyalty to their families. They are highly intelligent, protective, and affectionate companions that form strong and lasting bonds with their human counterparts. Their loyalty is a defining characteristic that sets them apart, making them a sought-after choice for families in search of a devoted and reliable pet. With their unwavering loyalty, Dobermans bring immense joy and a deep sense of companionship to the lives of their owners.

Here are some of the ways that Doberman dogs exhibit their loyalty towards their family:

1. **Protective Nature:** Dobermans are renowned for their innate protectiveness towards their families. They possess a natural instinct to guard their loved

ones and will readily react to any perceived threats. With their keen senses and watchful nature, Dobermans make excellent guard dogs and provide a sense of security to their households.

2. **Affectionate Companionship:** Dobermans are deeply affectionate dogs that form strong emotional bonds with their families. They thrive on human companionship and enjoy being in the company of their loved ones. They are known to shower their owners with love and attention, often seeking closeness and physical contact.

3. **Reliability and Support:** Dobermans are dependable and loyal companions, always ready to provide support and comfort to their family members. They possess an intuitive understanding of their owners' emotions and can offer solace during challenging times. Their unwavering presence and loyalty make them a reliable source of support and companionship.

4. **Trainability:** Dobermans are renowned for their high trainability and willingness to learn. They possess remarkable intelligence and are quick learners, making them an ideal choice for training. Whether it's

mastering basic obedience commands or engaging in more complex tasks, Dobermans excel in various training activities and are eager to please their owners.

5. **Adaptability:** Dobermans are adaptable dogs that can thrive in different living situations and environments. They can easily adjust to urban or rural settings and can accommodate both apartment living and larger homes. Their loyalty and devotion to their family remain steadfast, regardless of the surroundings or challenges they encounter.

Dobermans' exceptional trainability and adaptability make them versatile companions for individuals and families alike. Their eagerness to learn and their ability to adapt to different lifestyles and environments contribute to their reputation as intelligent and highly adaptable canine companions.

How Dobermans Can Provide Protection for Their Families

Doberman Pinschers are widely recognized for their

unwavering loyalty and fearless nature, positioning them as exceptional guardians of their families. We will delve into the ways in which Dobermans offer protection to their families and why they are a remarkable choice for individuals who prioritize safety and security.

Innate protective instincts: Dobermans possess innate protective instincts ingrained in their breeding history. They are naturally alert and vigilant, always keeping an eye out for any potential dangers. With an inherent drive to safeguard their family, Dobermans excel as watchdogs, utilizing their high energy levels and need for exercise to maintain a constant state of readiness.

Impressive presence and deterrence: With their muscular and commanding physique, Dobermans exude a strong and intimidating presence. Their sleek and elegant appearance, combined with their imposing stature, serves as a deterrent to would-be intruders. The sheer physical strength of Dobermans enables them to physically restrain intruders, providing a formidable defense until help arrives.

Swift response capabilities: Dobermans possess remarkable agility and speed, allowing them to respond swiftly to potential threats. They possess a natural ability to react promptly, covering large distances in a short period of time. This agility and quick response time make them an optimal choice for individuals seeking a dog that can promptly identify and address potential dangers.

Loyalty and specialized protection training: Dobermans exhibit unwavering loyalty towards their family and can be trained to respond to specific commands and cues, enhancing their protective abilities. Through targeted training, they can develop the skills to discern between friendly and hostile individuals, providing an added layer of security. This specialized training empowers Dobermans to serve as reliable protectors of their family's well-being.

Emotional support and reassurance: In addition to their protective instincts, Dobermans offer valuable emotional support to their family members. The deep bond formed between a Doberman and its owner is renowned for its strength and devotion. This emotional connection provides a sense of comfort and assurance, ensuring that the family feels safe and secure with their loyal and affectionate companion always by their side.

In conclusion, Doberman Pinschers are an outstanding choice for individuals seeking a reliable family protector.

Their innate instincts, formidable appearance, swift response capabilities, loyalty, and specialized protection training, as well as their ability to provide emotional support, position them as an ideal breed for those prioritizing safety and security. With proper training and care, Dobermans offer unparalleled protection and unwavering companionship to their beloved family members.

Health and Maintenance

Doberman Pinschers are generally a healthy breed with a lifespan of around 10 to 13 years. However, like all dogs, they are prone to certain health issues that owners should be aware of. Regular veterinary check-ups, vaccinations, and preventive care are crucial for maintaining their overall well-being.

Some common health concerns in Dobermans include dilated cardiomyopathy (a heart condition), hip dysplasia, von Willebrand's disease (a bleeding disorder), and hypothyroidism. It's important to work closely with a reputable breeder who conducts health screenings to minimize the risk of these inherited conditions.

Chapter 4:
Common Health Issues for Dobermans

Doberman Pinschers are cherished for their intelligence, loyalty, and athleticism. However, it's important for owners to be aware of the potential health issues that can affect this breed. Regular veterinary care and proactive maintenance are essential for ensuring the well-being of Dobermans. The following are common health issues of this breed:

1. Dilated Cardiomyopathy (DCM)

Dilated cardiomyopathy (DCM) is a heart condition that can affect Dobermans. It involves the enlargement and weakening of the heart, potentially leading to heart failure. Recognizing the symptoms of DCM, such as lethargy, coughing, and breathing difficulties, is crucial for early intervention. While there is currently no cure for DCM, timely detection and appropriate treatment can help manage the symptoms and improve the dog's quality of life. Regular check-ups and monitoring by a veterinarian are essential to ensure the well-being of Dobermans and address any potential health issues promptly.

2. Von Willebrand's Disease (VWD)

Von Willebrand Disease (VWD) is a blood clotting disorder that is prevalent in Dobermans. It occurs due to a deficiency in the protein responsible for blood clotting. Recognizing the symptoms of VWD, such as excessive bleeding, bruising, and prolonged bleeding after injury or surgery, is crucial for early intervention. While there is currently no known cure for VWD, the condition can be effectively managed through medication and close monitoring. Regular check-ups with a veterinarian, along with appropriate precautions during medical procedures, can help ensure the well-being of Dobermans affected by VWD.

3. Hip Dysplasia

Hip dysplasia is a hereditary condition that commonly affects the hip joints of Dobermans. It can lead to discomfort, lameness, and the development of arthritis in affected dogs. To address hip dysplasia, various measures can be taken, including the use of medication, weight management, and surgical intervention in severe cases. Regular exercise that avoids excessive strain on the hips, along with a balanced diet, can help maintain the overall health and well-being of Dobermans prone to hip dysplasia. Regular veterinary check-ups and consultations are essential for monitoring and managing this condition effectively.

4. Wobbler Syndrome

Wobbler Syndrome is a spinal condition that specifically affects Dobermans. It is characterized by the compression of the spinal cord, resulting in symptoms such as weakness, lack of coordination, and potential paralysis in affected dogs. While there is no known cure for Wobbler Syndrome, the condition can be managed through a combination of medication and, in severe cases, surgical intervention. Close monitoring and regular veterinary care are essential to ensure the well-being and quality of life of Dobermans with Wobbler Syndrome.

5. Hypothyroidism

Hypothyroidism is a hormonal disorder that can occur in Dobermans. It is characterized by inadequate production of thyroid hormones, which can result in symptoms such as weight gain, lethargy, and skin issues in affected dogs.

Fortunately, hypothyroidism can be effectively managed through medication, dietary adjustments, and consistent monitoring. With proper treatment and ongoing veterinary care, Dobermans with hypothyroidism can lead happy and healthy lives.

6. Bloat

Bloat, also known as gastric dilatation-volvulus (GDV), is a serious and potentially life-threatening condition that can affect Dobermans. It occurs when the stomach becomes twisted, resulting in a blockage in the digestive system. If left untreated, bloat can lead to shock and even death. It is crucial to recognize the symptoms of bloat, such as restlessness, pacing, and a swollen abdomen. Immediate veterinary attention is necessary to alleviate the condition. Preventive measures, such as implementing proper feeding practices and avoiding vigorous exercise before and after meals, can help reduce the risk of bloat in Dobermans.

In conclusion, while Dobermans are indeed a wonderful breed of dog, it is crucial for owners to acknowledge and be proactive about the common health issues that can affect them. By staying informed and working closely with their veterinarian, owners can provide the best care and support for their beloved Dobermans. With proper attention, care, and management, Dobermans can thrive and enjoy long, healthy lives as cherished members of their families.

Tips for Maintaining Your Doberman's Health

Doberman Pinschers are intelligent and active dogs that require regular exercise, a nutritious diet, and proper healthcare to maintain their health and well-being. Here are some tips to help you keep your Doberman healthy:

- ❖ **Regular Veterinary Check-ups:** Make sure to schedule regular check-ups with your veterinarian for your Doberman. Aim for at least one annual visit, but more frequent visits may be necessary for puppies and older dogs. These check-ups allow the vet to monitor your dog's overall health, catch any potential issues early, and provide necessary preventive care such as vaccinations, parasite control, and dental examinations.

- ❖ **Balanced and Nutritious Diet:** Provide your Doberman with a well-balanced and nutritious diet. Choose a high-quality dog food that is appropriate for their age, size, and activity level. Look for formulas that contain essential nutrients, such as protein, healthy fats, vitamins, and minerals. Avoid feeding your Doberman table scraps or unhealthy human foods, as these can lead to weight gain, digestive issues, and nutritional imbalances. It is important to note that Dobermans generally do well with diets that include grains, so opt for a quality diet that includes grains rather than a grain-free diet.

- **Regular Exercise:** Dobermans are an energetic and active breed that requires regular exercise to maintain their physical and mental well-being. Engage your Doberman in daily exercise routines such as brisk walks, jogging, playtime, or activities like agility training. Exercise not only helps to keep them physically fit but also provides mental stimulation and helps prevent behavioral issues that may arise from pent-up energy.

- **Dental Care:** Good oral hygiene is essential for your Doberman's overall health. Establish a regular dental care routine that includes brushing your dog's teeth with dog-friendly toothpaste, providing dental chews or toys for chewing, and considering professional dental cleanings as recommended by your veterinarian. Proper dental care helps prevent dental disease, bad breath, and other oral health problems.

- **Socialization and Training:** Socialization and training are crucial for the well-rounded development of your Doberman. Expose them to different environments, people, and animals from a young age. Enroll them in puppy classes or obedience training to learn basic commands and manners. Positive reinforcement methods work well with Dobermans, as they are eager to please and respond well to praise and rewards.

- **Mental Stimulation:** Engage your Doberman's mind with interactive toys, puzzle games, and training sessions. Mental stimulation is just as important as physical exercise and helps prevent boredom and destructive behaviors. Teach them new tricks, provide challenging toys, or consider activities like nose work or obedience competitions to keep their minds sharp and active.

- **Environmental Hazards:** It is crucial to be aware of potential environmental hazards that could pose a risk to your Doberman's health and safety. Take precautions to protect your dog from toxic plants, harmful chemicals, and extreme temperatures. Let's discuss a little more about these environmental hazards:

1. **Toxic Plants:** Educate yourself about common plants that are toxic to dogs and ensure they are not present in your home or yard. Some examples include lilies, azaleas, and certain types of ferns. If you suspect your Doberman has ingested a toxic plant, contact your veterinarian immediately.

2. **Chemicals and Household Substances:** Keep household chemicals, cleaning products, and medications securely stored in areas that are inaccessible to your Doberman. Many common household substances can be toxic if ingested, so it's essential to prevent accidental exposure.

3. **Extreme Temperatures:** Dobermans are sensitive to extreme temperatures. During hot weather, provide ample shade and fresh water to prevent overheating. Avoid leaving your

Doberman in a parked car, as temperatures can rise rapidly and cause heatstroke. In cold weather, provide a warm and sheltered area for your dog, and consider using dog clothing or blankets to help them stay comfortable.

Chapter 5:

Doberman Breeding

The breeding of Dobermans is a meticulous process that aims to produce dogs with desirable physical traits, temperament, and health. Dobermans, formally known as Doberman Pinschers, is a distinct and recognizable breed known for their elegance, loyalty, and intelligence. This short introduction will provide a glimpse into the world of Doberman breeding, highlighting the considerations and objectives involved in creating and maintaining this beloved breed.

Breed Characteristics

The Doberman is a breed of dog that is known for its striking appearance, athleticism, intelligence, and loyalty. Developed in the late 19th century by Karl Friedrich Louis Dobermann, this breed possesses a distinct set of characteristics that make it stand out among other dog breeds. In this section, we will delve into the various breed characteristics of the Doberman.

Appearance:

The Doberman is a medium to large-sized breed with a well-muscled and compact build. They have a sleek, short coat that comes in a variety of colors, including black, blue, red, and fawn. Their coat is low-maintenance and requires minimal grooming. One of the most recognizable features of the Doberman is its alert and expressive face, with almond-shaped eyes and cropped ears (although ear cropping is becoming less common in many countries). They have a confident and powerful stance, reflecting their athletic abilities.

Temperament:

Dobermans are renowned for their loyal and protective nature. They are devoted to their families and form strong bonds with their owners. They have a natural instinct to protect and guard, which makes them excellent watchdogs. With proper socialization and training, Dobermans can be friendly, gentle, and affectionate. However, they also have an assertive side and can be reserved or wary of strangers. Early socialization is essential to ensure they develop into well-rounded and confident dogs.

Intelligence:

The Doberman is highly intelligent and ranks among the most intelligent dog breeds. They are quick learners and have a strong desire to please their owners. This intelligence, combined with their eagerness to learn, makes them highly trainable. They excel in obedience, agility, and other dog sports. Mental stimulation is crucial for Dobermans to prevent boredom and destructive behavior, as they thrive when given tasks to solve or challenges to overcome.

Energy and Exercise:

Dobermans are an active and energetic breed. They require regular exercise to maintain their physical and mental well-being. Daily walks, runs, or play sessions are necessary to keep them physically fit and prevent pent-up energy that may lead to behavioral issues. Engaging in activities such as fetch, agility training, or obedience training can help channel their energy and provide mental stimulation. However, it is important to avoid excessive exercise, especially in hot weather, as Dobermans are prone to overheating.

Trainability:

Dobermans are known for their trainability and responsiveness to commands. They thrive in structured and consistent training environments. Positive reinforcement techniques, such as rewards, praise, and treats, work exceptionally well with this breed. They are sensitive to their owner's tone and body language, making them attentive and receptive during training sessions. Early socialization is crucial to ensure they grow up to be well-mannered and adaptable in various environments.

Health:

Like many breeds, Dobermans have certain health considerations. Some common health issues in Dobermans, as discussed in the previous chapter, include hip dysplasia, von Willebrand's disease, dilated cardiomyopathy, and thyroid problems. Reputable breeders conduct health screenings and genetic testing to reduce the incidence of these issues in their breeding programs. Regular veterinary check-ups, a balanced diet, and exercise, are essential for maintaining the overall health and longevity of Dobermans.

In summary, the Doberman breed possesses a unique set of characteristics that combine intelligence, loyalty, athleticism, and a protective nature. With the right upbringing, socialization, and training, Dobermans make devoted family companions, versatile working dogs, and impressive competitors in various dog sports. Their distinctive appearance and unwavering loyalty have made them beloved companions for countless individuals and families worldwide.

Popularity and Recognition

Doberman Pinschers have gained significant popularity and recognition as a breed over the years. Known for their sleek appearance, intelligence, and loyalty, they have captured the attention of dog enthusiasts worldwide. Let's delve into the factors that have contributed to the popularity and recognition of Doberman Pinschers.

Striking Appearance:

One of the primary reasons for the breed's popularity is its striking appearance. With their muscular build, elegant lines, and sleek coat, Doberman Pinschers exude a sense of power and athleticism. Their alert expression, coupled with their distinctive markings, particularly the black and tan coloration, adds to their visual appeal. The breed's physical presence has made them a sought-after choice for those looking for a visually impressive dog.

Versatility and Trainability:

Doberman Pinschers are known for their versatility and trainability. They excel in various activities and roles, including obedience, agility, tracking, search and rescue, and even therapy work. Their intelligence and eagerness to please make them quick learners, allowing them to succeed in different training endeavors. Their versatility has made them popular among individuals and families looking for a dog that can participate in various activities and fulfill different roles.

Loyalty and Protective Nature:

Dobermans are renowned for their loyalty and protective instincts. They form strong bonds with their owners and are dedicated to their families. This loyalty, combined with their natural guarding abilities, has made them popular choices for personal protection and home security. Their ability to be both loving family members and reliable protectors has garnered them recognition and popularity among those seeking a devoted and reliable companion.

Recognized by Kennel Clubs:

Doberman Pinschers are officially recognized and registered by prominent kennel clubs worldwide. Organizations such as the American Kennel Club (AKC), the Kennel Club (UK), the Federation Cynologique Internationale (FCI), and the Continental Kennel Club (CKC) have established breed standards and provide official recognition to Dobermans. This recognition ensures breed consistency and promotes responsible breeding practices, further enhancing the breed's reputation and popularity.

Success in Competitive Events:

Doberman Pinschers have achieved significant success in various competitive events, including conformation shows, obedience trials, and agility competitions. Their athleticism, intelligence, and trainability make them formidable competitors in these arenas. Winning titles and accolades in such events not only showcases the breed's abilities but also increases their visibility and recognition among dog enthusiasts and the general public.

Pop Culture Representation:

Doberman Pinschers have been featured in various forms of media, including movies, TV shows, and advertisements. Their imposing appearance and reputation as loyal and protective dogs have made them popular choices for roles in film and television. These representations in pop culture have further solidified their image and contributed to their recognition and popularity.

In conclusion, Doberman Pinschers have gained popularity and recognition due to their striking appearance, versatility, trainability, loyalty, and protective nature. Their success in competitive events, recognition by kennel clubs, and representation in pop culture have also played a significant role. Whether as companions, working dogs, or show competitors, Doberman Pinschers have carved out a place for themselves as a highly regarded breed among dog lovers worldwide.

Chapter 6:
Training and Socialization

Training and socialization are essential aspects of raising a well-behaved and balanced Doberman. In this section, we will explore the importance of training and socialization for Dobermans, as well as provide useful tips and techniques to help you establish a strong bond with your canine companion. By investing time and effort into training and socializing your Doberman, you can ensure they become a confident, obedient, and well-adjusted member of your family.

Importance of Training and Socialization for Dobermans

Dobermans are renowned for their intelligence and loyalty, making proper training and socialization crucial for their well-being. In this chapter, we will delve into the significance of training and socialization for Dobermans and their owners.

Training plays a vital role in responsible dog ownership. It encompasses teaching dogs to comprehend and follow commands, exhibit appropriate behavior in various situations, and respond effectively. Given the intelligence and strength of Dobermans, training is of utmost importance and necessitates a firm and consistent approach.

One of the key advantages of training is the establishment of a strong bond between owners and their Dobermans. Training sessions provide opportunities for positive reinforcement, fostering trust and strengthening the relationship between both parties. This bond is particularly valuable for Dobermans, renowned for their unwavering loyalty and devotion to their owners.

Training is highly beneficial in fostering a strong bond between owners and their dogs. By engaging in training sessions, positive reinforcement becomes a cornerstone, enhancing trust and deepening the relationship. This connection holds particular significance for Dobermans, renowned for their unparalleled loyalty and devotion to their owners.

Moreover, training plays a pivotal role in preventing behavior problems. As Dobermans possess a natural protectiveness, proper socialization and training are vital to curb aggression. Obedience training equips them with the ability to respond to commands and manage their impulses, minimizing the likelihood of dangerous behavior.

In addition to training, socialization is a critical component of responsible dog ownership. Socialization entails exposing dogs to people, other canines, and diverse environments, enabling them to learn appropriate interaction. Given the strong protective instinct and territorial nature of Dobermans, socialization is particularly imperative for them.

Proper socialization plays a crucial role in reducing fear and anxiety in Dobermans. By exposing them to various people, animals, and environments, socialization fosters a sense of comfort and confidence in unfamiliar situations. Moreover, it helps prevent aggressive behavior towards strangers and other dogs.

Initiating training and socialization early in a Doberman's life is paramount. Puppy training classes serve as an excellent starting point for instilling basic commands and facilitating interaction with fellow puppies and humans within a structured environment.

In addition to formal training classes, ongoing training, and socialization should be prioritized throughout a Doberman's lifetime. Regular exercise and playtime are essential to keep Dobermans physically and mentally stimulated. Introducing interactive toys and puzzles provides mental engagement and serves as a preventive measure against boredom and destructive behaviors.

In conclusion, the importance of proper training and socialization cannot be overstated for Dobermans and their owners. Through training, a strong bond is formed between the owner and the dog, behavioral issues are prevented, and impulse control is developed. Socialization plays a vital role in reducing fear and anxiety, preventing aggression, and exposing Dobermans to diverse people and environments. By prioritizing training and socialization, Dobermans can become loyal, well-behaved, and adaptable members of the family.

Effective Training and Socialization Methods

Proper training and socialization are essential for the well-being and happiness of Dobermans. We will explore effective methods for training and socializing Dobermans, helping them become well-behaved, confident, and balanced dogs. These effective methods are discussed below:

Positive Reinforcement

Positive reinforcement is a highly effective training method that focuses on rewarding desirable behavior in Dobermans. By using treats, verbal praise, and playtime as rewards, owners can create a positive association between the desired behavior and the rewards. Dobermans are known to respond well to positive reinforcement, as they are highly motivated by treats and praise. This approach encourages their willingness to learn and reinforces their good behavior.

Consistency

Consistency plays a vital role in effective training for Dobermans. By using consistent commands and rewards, owners can prevent confusion and frustration in their dogs. Dobermans, being intelligent and responsive to structure, benefit greatly from consistent training methods. Using the same commands and rewards consistently helps them understand and meet the expectations set for them. By maintaining a consistent approach, owners can provide clear guidance to their Dobermans and facilitate their learning process effectively.

Socialization

Socialization plays a vital role in the development of Dobermans, ensuring their comfort in various situations and environments. It involves gradually introducing the dog to new people, animals, and environments in a positive and controlled manner. Early and ongoing socialization is crucial for Dobermans to build confidence and adaptability. By exposing them to diverse experiences from a young age, owners can help them develop into well-rounded and sociable dogs. Continued socialization throughout their lives ensures that Dobermans remain comfortable and at ease in different situations they may encounter.

Desensitization

Desensitization is a valuable training technique that helps dogs overcome fear and anxiety towards specific stimuli. It involves controlled and gradual exposure to the feared stimulus, such as loud noises or other dogs, with the aim of reducing the dog's negative response. By slowly introducing the stimulus in a positive and controlled manner and pairing it with rewards or positive experiences, desensitization can help the dog become more comfortable and confident in the presence of previously feared triggers. This method allows the dog to build resilience and develop a more positive association with the once-frightening stimuli.

Clicker Training

Clicker training is an effective and positive reinforcement method used to train Dobermans. It involves utilizing a clicker, which emits a distinct sound, to mark the desired behavior. The sound of the clicker serves as an immediate and precise signal to the dog, indicating that they have performed the desired action correctly. This clear communication allows for efficient training and enables Dobermans to understand and associate their actions with rewards. Clicker training is particularly suitable for Dobermans due to their intelligence and ability to grasp concepts quickly, making it a valuable tool in their structured training process.

Playtime

Playtime plays a vital role in the training and socialization of Dobermans. It offers an opportunity for dogs to engage with their owners and other dogs in a controlled and positive setting. During playtime, dogs receive both mental and physical stimulation, which is crucial for their overall well-being.

In conclusion, the well-being and happiness of Dobermans heavily rely on effective training and socialization. Employing methods such as positive reinforcement, consistency, socialization, desensitization, clicker training, and incorporating regular playtime can result in well-adjusted and content Dobermans. By utilizing these techniques, owners can establish a strong bond with their dogs and ensure they become valued members of the family.

Chapter 7:

Misconceptions and Controversies Surrounding Dobermans

Misconceptions and controversies surrounding Dobermans have led to misunderstandings and stereotypes about this beloved breed. In this chapter, we will address and debunk some of the common misconceptions and controversies surrounding Dobermans. By shedding light on these topics, we aim to provide a more accurate and informed understanding of Dobermans and their true nature.

Common Misconceptions

Doberman dogs have often been unfairly labeled as aggressive guard dogs, resulting in various misconceptions about the breed. In this chapter, we will explore and debunk some of these common misconceptions surrounding Dobermans. By dispelling these misconceptions, we aim to provide a more accurate understanding of the true nature of Doberman dogs.

Dobermans Are Aggressive

One prevalent misconception about Dobermans is their presumed innate aggression. However, it is important to note that Dobermans are not inherently aggressive dogs. While they possess a protective nature towards their owners, proper training and socialization play a crucial role in shaping their behavior. With appropriate guidance, Dobermans can exhibit loyalty, affection, and a gentle disposition towards their owners and others.

Dobermans Are Not Good With Children

Another misconception surrounding Dobermans is the belief that they are not suitable for households with children. However, when raised and trained appropriately, Dobermans can make wonderful family companions. Early socialization and training are key to fostering a gentle and affectionate nature in Dobermans towards children. It is important to supervise interactions between children and dogs of any breed to ensure a safe and harmonious environment for both. With the right guidance and care, Dobermans can form loving bonds with children and become cherished family members.

Dobermans are Difficult to Train

Dobermans are renowned for their high intelligence and capacity to learn, making them receptive to positive reinforcement training techniques. Although they can display stubborn tendencies on occasion, consistent and patient training methods can yield remarkable results. The misconception that Dobermans are challenging to train may arise from their independent nature and innate protective instincts. However, with appropriate training and socialization,

Dobermans can develop into well-mannered and obedient companions.

Dobermans Need A Lot of Exercise

While Dobermans are indeed energetic and athletic, they do not require excessive amounts of exercise. Regular exercise and engaging play sessions, coupled with mental stimulation, are vital for the overall well-being of Dobermans. However, it is important to avoid over-exercising these dogs as it can have negative consequences and contribute to health issues. Striking the right balance by providing appropriate exercise and mental stimulation is key to keeping Dobermans healthy and happy.

Dobermans Are Not Good With Other Pets

Dobermans have the potential to peacefully coexist with other pets when they receive proper socialization and training. While they may possess a high prey drive, this instinct can be managed through training and close supervision. With the right approach, Dobermans can be taught to live harmoniously with cats and other small animals.

In conclusion, Doberman dogs often face misconceptions stemming from their reputation as aggressive guard dogs. It is important to debunk these misconceptions, such as the belief that they are inherently aggressive, unsuitable for children or other pets, difficult to train, or in need of excessive exercise. By providing appropriate training and socialization, Dobermans can exhibit well-mannered behavior and display affectionate qualities as beloved family dogs.

Controversies Surrounding Dobermans

Dobermans have been embroiled in numerous controversies and criticisms since their inception in the late 19th century. One of the most prominent issues surrounds their health problems, which are known to be prevalent within the breed. Concerns such as hip dysplasia, von Willebrand's disease, and dilated cardiomyopathy have raised eyebrows. Critics argue that these health issues stem from inbreeding and a focus on physical appearance at the expense of overall health. As a result, there have been appeals for more responsible breeding practices and genetic testing to minimize the occurrence of these ailments in Dobermans.

Another significant controversy surrounding Dobermans revolves around their perceived aggression. This reputation can be attributed to their historical role as guard dogs and their innate protective instincts. However, with proper training and socialization, Dobermans can demonstrate gentleness and affection as family pets. Unfortunately, some irresponsible owners may encourage or train their Dobermans to display aggressive behavior, leading to incidents and negative media attention. This has prompted calls for enhanced owner education and stricter regulations to prevent such occurrences.

Dobermans have faced bans or restrictions in certain countries, such as Germany, the United Kingdom, and parts of Australia. These measures stem from the breed's reputation as an aggressive guard dog and concerns about public safety. However, animal welfare organizations and experts criticize breed-specific legislation for its ineffectiveness in addressing dog-related incidents and failure to target the underlying causes. Instead, they advocate for more comprehensive legislation that emphasizes responsible dog ownership and the prevention of such incidents.

In addition, the practices of ear cropping and tail docking have sparked controversy within the Doberman community. Ear cropping involves altering the shape of the dog's ears for aesthetic purposes, while tail docking involves removing the dog's tail. These practices are deemed illegal in several countries, including the United Kingdom, Australia, and parts of Europe. Critics argue that these procedures are unnecessary, inflict pain on the animals, and should only be performed for legitimate medical reasons. Although some countries still permit ear cropping and tail docking for show dogs, there has been a decline in their prevalence in recent years.

In conclusion, Dobermans have been surrounded by various controversies, encompassing health concerns, aggression, breed-specific legislation, and the contentious practices of ear cropping and tail docking. It is crucial to approach these controversies with a discerning perspective while prioritizing the welfare of the breed and individual dogs. By implementing responsible breeding practices, as well as providing proper training and socialization, many of these issues can be effectively addressed, leading to well-behaved and healthy Dobermans that can thrive as valued members of the family.

Conclusion

Recap of the Reasons Why Dobermans Make the Best Family Dogs

Throughout this book, we have explored the many reasons why Dobermans make excellent family dogs. In this chapter, we will summarize the key points and reiterate why Dobermans are the perfect addition to any family.

Firstly, Dobermans possess a variety of desirable characteristics that make them great family dogs. They are strong, agile, and athletic, making them ideal for families who enjoy an active lifestyle. Their short, sleek coat is easy to maintain, which is ideal for busy families. In terms of temperament, Dobermans are intelligent, loyal, and affectionate dogs who form strong bonds with their families. They have a natural protective instinct, which makes them an excellent watchdog and an effective deterrent against intruders.

Secondly, Dobermans have a special affinity with children due to their patient and gentle nature. They have a natural instinct to protect, and this extends to the younger members of the family. Dobermans are known for their tolerance towards children's unpredictable behavior, making them a great choice for families. They understand that children may be playful and even a little rough at times, and they have the patience and understanding to handle it with grace. Their playful and energetic nature also complements the active lifestyles of children, as they can keep up with their energy levels and provide a fun and engaging playmate. This interaction not only keeps children entertained but also helps foster a strong bond between them.

Additionally, Dobermans have shown exceptional capabilities as therapy dogs, further highlighting their ability to connect with people. Their inherent loyalty and empathy make them well-suited for providing comfort and emotional support to individuals in need. Whether it's visiting hospitals, nursing homes or participating in animal-assisted therapy programs, Dobermans have proven to be gentle and understanding companions. Their presence alone can bring joy and a sense of calm to those they interact with, making them invaluable in therapeutic settings.

Furthermore, Dobermans are renowned for their unwavering loyalty and protective instincts towards their families. They form deep attachments and will go to great lengths to ensure the safety and well-being of their loved ones. With a Doberman by your side, you can have peace of mind knowing that they will always be there to protect you and your home. Their alertness and natural instincts make them excellent watchdogs, deterring potential threats and alerting their owners to any unusual activity. Their devotion and protective nature create a strong sense of security, allowing you to feel safe and protected in their presence.

Finally, Dobermans are generally a healthy breed, requiring minimal veterinary care compared to some other breeds. They have a lifespan of around 10 to 12 years, and with proper care, they can enjoy a long and healthy life. Regular exercise, a balanced diet, routine vaccinations, and periodic check-ups with a veterinarian are all essential in maintaining their overall well-being. While no breed is entirely free from health concerns, Dobermans are relatively robust and not predisposed to many hereditary ailments. By providing them with a loving home, proper nutrition, regular exercise, and routine healthcare, you can help ensure that your Doberman remains healthy, happy, and by your side for many years to come.

In conclusion, Dobermans' affinity for children, loyalty, protective instincts, and general good health make them a popular and highly regarded breed. Their ability to form strong bonds with children, their natural protective instincts, and their overall health make them an excellent choice for families seeking a loyal, loving, and trustworthy companion. Dobermans have proven time and again that they have the temperament and qualities to be not only a beloved family pet but also a source of unwavering loyalty, protection, and joy.

Final Thoughts and Recommendations for Potential Doberman Owners

If you are considering getting a Doberman as a family dog, there are a few final thoughts and recommendations to keep in mind. These will help ensure that you are fully prepared for life with this amazing breed and can provide them with the care and environment they need to thrive.

Firstly, it is important to understand that Dobermans require a significant amount of attention and exercise. They have a high energy level and are an active breed that requires daily physical activity to keep them healthy and happy. This means that as a potential owner, you should be ready to commit to regular exercise routines such as daily walks, jogs, or playtime in a secure and spacious area. Providing them with ample opportunities to release their energy and engage in stimulating activities will contribute to their overall well-being.

Secondly, training and socialization are crucial for Dobermans. While they are intelligent and trainable, they also have a strong will and need proper guidance to become well-behaved companions. Early socialization and obedience training are essential to help them develop good manners, interact positively with people and other animals, and navigate various environments. It is recommended to enroll your Doberman in puppy classes or seek professional training assistance to ensure they receive the proper guidance and structure they need to grow into well-adjusted dogs.

Thirdly, it's important to consider the financial aspect of owning a Doberman. While they are generally healthy dogs, routine veterinary care is necessary to keep them in optimal health. This includes regular check-ups, vaccinations, and preventative measures against common health issues. Additionally, providing them with high-quality food, appropriate grooming, and necessary supplies will contribute to their overall well-being and happiness. Budgeting for these expenses is essential to ensure that you can provide the best care for your Doberman.

Finally, it is crucial to consider whether a Doberman is the right breed for your family and lifestyle. While they make excellent family dogs, their natural protective instincts can make them cautious or wary around strangers. This characteristic can be an asset for some households, but it is essential to consider how it aligns with your family's needs and preferences. Additionally, their high energy level requires an active and engaging lifestyle, so if your family prefers a more low-key or sedentary lifestyle, a Doberman may not be the best fit.

In conclusion, Dobermans are wonderful family dogs, but potential owners should be fully prepared to provide them with the attention, exercise, and training they require. With the right care and commitment, Dobermans become loyal, loving, and protective companions that will make them cherished members of your family. Before bringing a Doberman into your home, take the time to do thorough research, consult with experienced breeders or owners, and ensure that this breed aligns with your lifestyle, expectations, and ability to meet their needs. By making an informed decision and providing proper care, you can have a fulfilling and rewarding experience with your Doberman companion.